NAKEIA

I hope this helps

NAKEIA HOMER

I hope this helps

For Madis Myers, *Always & Forever*

and

George Myers III, *Hey, hey, hey...*

I've been here before.

Lost. Confused. Depressed. And in desperate
need of something better.

I need to know what to do, how to feel,
what to expect, and how to find my way
back to myself.

People are speaking…

Words are spoken…

But I hear nothing. I feel nothing.

So… what do I do when the words of the
ones who know and love me aren't enough?

How do I find my way back?

I write. I write the words I need to hear.

-Lost and Found

From the Author

Here I am.

Not far from where I used to be, but far
enough to see the change. If I really need
to, I can reach back and grab a lesson or two.
And believe me I really need to, often.

That's the thing about life: sometimes it
makes no sense until it makes sense.

I remember being 9 years old, living in the
projects, and demanding answers. I had
evening chats with God. I would ask him to
give a good reason for me to be living with
my grandmom and not my mom (like my
little sister.) I wanted a reason for loved ones
being addicted to drugs. I wanted answers as
to why we didn't have money, why the car
would break down all the time, and why I
always felt so darn bad.

It wasn't until I was well into my twenties
that I realized the answer. I say this with
certainty and anxiety- but the answer was
simple: to make me better.

I remember saying early in life that I didn't want to learn anything the hard way. I heard Oprah say, "I like to learn from other people's mistakes." And I felt that. I don't *need* the hard lessons, but I've had many.

Anxiety tries to creep back in at the thought of all the lessons I have yet to learn. I have more work to do. But I know, for sure, that every circumstance in life (good and bad) serves as an opportunity to become better- and I wanted better.

The minute I stopped running from the lessons my life would have me learn, I felt a shift. I would rise to the occasion of each circumstance and be lifted every time. Now, instead of being held down by the weight of the process, I flow through it.

When I feel anxious, I have more chats with God. I always leave those conversations with words that help me on my journey from one lesson to the next.

Now, I have the opportunity to share those words with you.

I hope it helps.

How This Reads

I hope this helps

Life.

Here you are.

How you ended up here isn't important, right now. When you find your way back, you'll have plenty of time to reflect. And when you do, the first thing that will catch your eye is the lesson.

Always look for the lesson.

Sometimes your circumstances will cause you to see life as a battle.

You may wake up and immediately prepare for a fight. Your protective gear is on your nightstand. You grab it before starting your day. You recite your daily mantras, internally, while brushing your teeth.

"Why does *my* life have to be so hard?"

"I can handle this on my own. I don't need anyone else."

"I'm so tired of <u>this</u> and <u>that</u>...but it's okay. I'll be alright."

Up to this point, life has been a crazy mess. You're tired of fighting.

I say, stop fighting.

Life gets crazier the more you resist. Go through the lesson with grace; and pick your strength up on the other side.

- The Battle

For a while, I thought I had the hardest life ever. I mean, I knew there were people experiencing *real* struggle, with *really* serious circumstances. Those people might look at me and see my life as easy, compared to theirs. But every life is different. Every struggle counts. No matter how hard or how long you have to fight, a fight is still a fight- and I was tired of fighting.

My fight started at birth, and that's no exaggeration. I had a 2 week stay in the NICU because of it. If you factor in having a 15 year old mother and a 17 year old father, one might say I started fighting at conception.

I was raised in the projects, by my paternal grandmother, exposed to all kinds of mess for the first 18 years of my life. I was no stranger to struggle. I was used to fighting. But I was tired.

I made intentional choices that got me out of the hood, helped me break the generational cycle of teenage pregnancy and earn a college degree. My choices kept me off drugs and alcohol and spared me the pain of abusive relationships. But still... I struggled.

Of course, I messed some things up. I've gone way too far into some other things. I needed life to get easier. I wanted everything to work out the first time. I wanted to avoid rejection, bypass any delays, and I wanted what I felt like I had earned–
Peace of mind.

I could go into detail about my broken heart, my failed business attempts, my kidney disease, my life with no money, my low self-esteem, my moments of betrayal, my this and my that. But you have details of your own this and your own that...so I don't have to tell you, life gets hard.

That is life.

I came to realize that *hard* doesn't have to be a curse. The hardest things I've ever had to face are also the same things that molded me into the woman I am today. I got here *through* struggle, *because* of struggle- not by avoiding it.

I am here. That means that I've won the fight.

I still get tired of fighting. But I never get tired of winning.

I am here. And how I got here has been my biggest blessing.

Was it a **broken heart**?

Was it a pink slip from your **dream job**?

Was it a new **marriage**?

Was it your *first born or unborn child*?

Was it a **broken promise**?

Was it your unexpected **diagnosis**?

Was it your **big idea**?

Was it a **decision** to do something different?

Whatever IT was that brought you to **this
point in life**- all of it- **was for your good**.

The moment you realize that, will also
be the moment you finally take that deep
breath and move forward with purpose.

-The Point of It All

I learned a long time ago that I will never win if I put myself in a ring with life.

Life is too big and too powerful to fight.

Instead, I sat down with life and had a long discussion about how I want to live it and what the rules were going to be.

At the end of that discussion, life and I became partners and together we found my purpose.

Your past is relevant when what you learn
from it helps you and someone else.
It is time that you learn from it.

Stop fighting it. At this point in your life, it
is what it is- not what it should be or what
you may want it to be. But that's
okay. Your life is not over. Just end the
fight. Take a moment to have the discussion.
Define the type of life you want to live and
how you plan to make it all happen.

Acknowledge the lessons. It is easy to
overlook the lesson that a difficult
circumstance can bring. Go back to the
moment you experienced your most difficult
circumstance and welcome the
lesson. Could you learn to listen to your
intuition more? Could you learn to be more
assertive and to give less of your power
away? Could you learn how to be a better
friend or a better love? Whatever lesson you
learn could be the one thing you needed to
take you to the next level.

Become a partner. When you learn to work with your life and not against it, you gain control over the type of life you want to live. Instead of life just happening to you and around you, life begins to happen for you. Nothing happens without your consent or awareness.

Yeah, she fell.

She got distracted, lost her direction, made some mistakes, broke some promises, forgot who she was...

But she got up.

She remembered who she was, gathered her thoughts, regained her focus, tightened up her hustle, and recovered.

The same people who saw her fall, will witness her come back.

Forgive yourself
for learning some things, the hard way.

This one is for the person who refuses to forgive themselves for getting hurt again.

For the person who felt like they should have known better.

For girl who is too embarrassed to admit what she's done (again.)

There are some things you just won't get the first time.

Some things you gotta see for yourself.

Some lessons won't come easy.

Don't regret anything you've learned from—even if you had to learn the hard way.

You've done it.

You've given yourself an excuse to behave badly, to be afraid, to give up too easily, to run and retreat, to settle, to grin and bear it, and to fail. Are you brave enough to admit it?

When you do those things- when you don't take control of the way pain affects you, you miss an opportunity to meet your true self.

Hidden underneath your pain is the *you* who could hold the title of:

Survivor
Overcomer
Teacher
Lover
Friend
Mother
Inspiration
Leader

You've been through so much. Don't you think you've earned it?

-Crown

Your pain can also be your biggest gain. It can be the thing that leads you to your purpose, ushers in your passion, and guides you to your destiny.

Pain is painful. But, overcoming it can be an inspiration.

-Lighten Up

Be done with letting people talk you out of
your purpose.

Most of the time, their talk isn't even about you.

It's about their limiting beliefs, unfulfilled dreams, lack of understanding, and difficulty accepting the fact that someone else just might make it happen.

Your purpose is yours.
Your dreams are yours.
Your goals are yours.
Your vision is yours.

It was divinely placed in your heart, and you have what it takes to make it happen.

Accept that some people will never understand, and do it anyway.

What you are facing, right now, is either a blessing or a lesson. Either way, you'll be better because of it.

Sometimes it just is what it is, and not what you want it to be.

Some things need to be solved.
Some things need to be accepted.

Knowing the difference will save you a lot of grief.

The people in your life will either push you to where you need to be or stand in the way.

Stop making room for stand-ins.

You need people who inspire you.

You need at least 1 person who's not afraid to challenge you and hold you accountable.

You need someone who will speak life to you, someone who will pray away the fear and doubt.

You need to be surrounded by people who are going places, people with a vision and the hustle to match.

No more place fillers.
No more stand ins.

Find some people you can make things happen with.

Life will have you thinking you can't be anyone other than who you've always been.

Lies.

You can always begin again.

You'll change when staying the same
becomes unbearable.

When the thought of where you are is
overshadowed by the thought of where you
could be, you'll change.

You'll change when the way things have
been becomes optional.

When you realize the potential in something
different is limitless and all you see is
possibility, you'll change.

You'll change when you're ready.
You'll change when you need to.
You'll change when see there is no use in
staying the same.

-A Word on Change

Take care of you.

Behind every dope woman is a story only
she can tell.

Never expect anyone to do for you what they have been unable or unwilling to do for themselves.

If they don't love themselves, they can't love you.

If they are not careful with themselves, they can't be careful with you.

If they don't want to love and care for you, you can't make them.

If they don't want to change for themselves, they won't change for you.

If they don't want better for themselves, they won't give you any better.

If they don't want to change and be better, you can't make them.

You see how that works?

It's not personal.

Want what you want, ask for it, and be
prepared to get it.

Most people don't get what they want not because they don't deserve it, but because they don't have the courage to ask for it.

Most people aren't sitting on dreams because they're lazy, but because they don't think they are worthy enough to experience it.

If you want it, you already have the capacity to create it in your life.

God gives you the desires of your heart.

You have the right to want what you want.

Ask for it and be prepared to get it.

It's not over.
You still have your breath.

Exhausted
Overwhelmed
Frustrated
Confused...

But not through.

As long as there is breath in your body,
it's not over.

Keep going (if you can.)

You've gone through too much to get this far only to settle.

You've gone through heart break
Disappointment
Setbacks
Sickness
Depression
Extreme doubt and fear...

And you're still standing.

Surely you can get through "this" too.

Don't stop.
Don't quit.
Don't give up.
Don't turn back.
Don't shrink.
Don't fall off...

And don't settle.

I am learning that there are some things you just gotta take to the chin.

No matter how long it took you, how many mistakes you've made, or how many detours you've experienced, you're here now.

You should be proud of that.

What you lost is not the best
you ever had.

You're strong enough.
You're tough enough.
You know what you're doing.
You have what it takes.
You got this.

...And when you think you can't, check
your record.

You always do.

Don't force.
Don't rush.
Don't chase.
Don't stress.

Every single think will work out.

Ease into your day knowing that what is for you is already yours.

And what is yours will not pass you by.

Even though it doesn't feel like it right now
You're going to end up exactly where you
need to be, with the people who love you
the most, doing what you were created to
do.

Until then, just keep going.

There will always be someone who doesn't
think you can.
Don't let it be you.

Trust the timing of it all.

You want it to happen when you're ready,
not when you're desperate.

It will happen when you're ready.
It will happen when you can handle it.
It will happen when you've healed.
It will happen when you've learned the lesson.

It will happen when you're wiser.
It will happen when you're open.
It will happen when you have everything in place.

It will happen when it's time.

Don't let your desperation rush you.

You're not too late.
You're not too old.
You haven't blown your chances.
Your time isn't up.

Purpose takes time.

I had a conversation with myself one
morning that went like this:

Who told you you had to do it by a certain
time, in a certain way, with certain people?

Your age does not determine your timeline.
your breath does.

As long as you are still breathing, you still
have time to do your thing.

Just because it hasn't happened yet
doesn't mean it never will.

Pay attention to what you are doing, what you are thinking, and who you are with when you are at your best.

and stay right there.

You need to be in a space that brings out the best in you.

A space that feels safe enough to release the purpose inside of you.

A space that cultivates who you will be, while accepting who you are right now.

You need to be where you are seen, heard, and felt.

You will know when you get there because you'll be doing what you love, and feeling well emotionally, physically, and spiritually.

You'll be surround by people who make you feel good about being you- and you won't want to be anywhere else.

What if what you want the most can't find you because you are dimming your own light, hiding your own magic, downplaying your own brilliance, and denying your own power?

Life responds to how you show up in the world.

Downplaying your dopeness...
Shrinking your personality...
And minimizing your talent...
Will get you nowhere, with nothing.

At some point you just gotta be okay with being who you are.

You are who God created you to be and nothing less.

Even under the circumstances you're in...
Even after the things you've survived...
Even while in the middle of your healing process...
Even while you are growing...

You are a dope individual, with a charming personality, and massive talent.

It's important to be humble.

But do your thing.

There are two types of people in this world:

Those who create generational curses.
Those who break generational curses.

It's time to choose a side.

Who you choose to love needs to be worth
the space they take up in your heart.

Sometimes we can elevate people to a place in our lives, give them full access to space in our hearts- and they ain't even worth it.

There's a lot of talk about knowing your worth. But we need to have conversations about calculating the worth of those we share our lives and hearts with, too.

Are they worth your time, your energy, your effort, your investment, your love?

Stop waiting for people to give you
permission, support you, and validate you.

You are enough without them.

Some people have you thinking you need them to succeed.

They have you thinking their permission, their support, and their validation is what makes you worthy.

They lied.
Stop believing them and start believing in yourself.

Believe in the call on your life.
Believe you were created for a purpose.
Believe that the life God gave you qualified you for the journey.

Your existence is all the permission you need.

You can fight tired.
You can fight scared.
You can even fight wounded.

But you can't fight empty.

Fill yourself up.

Crying doesn't make you weak.

The right people will see you.
The right people will hear you.
The right people will feel you.
The right people will do right by you.

Surround yourself with the right people.

Dear rejection,

Thanks for the heads up. Thanks for redirecting my focus. Thanks for showing me who's for me and who's not. Thanks for protecting me from things I didn't see coming. Thanks for teaching me to protect my heart. Thank you for reminding me that what is for me will not pass...

Finally, rejection, thanks for showing me the importance of not allowing myself to want anything or anyone that doesn't want me.

With Love,
Everyone who has ever been rejected.

Healing.

You are not lazy, unmotivated, or stuck.

After years of living your life in survival mode, you are exhausted.

There's a difference.

Have you ever been there?
Still tired after just waking up
On autopilot during the day
Tuning in and out of conversations
Feeling a way but don't know why?

I can recall being there at least twice.

The weight of my life, and the lives of
people I love the most, became too much
for me- and I found myself physically,
emotionally, and spiritually exhausted.

I didn't know it was emotional exhaustion at
first.

I thought I was lacking motivation. I
thought I had lost my way. I thought I was
being weak...

And trying to explain this to other people is
even more exhausting.

We are not meant to survive our way
through our entire lives. It is unfair to our
souls.

And when the weight of surviving becomes
too much, it is okay to stop, to rest, to
disconnect, to retreat, and to heal.

Ways to heal emotional exhaustion:

Set aside at least 1 night for a full (9 hours) night's sleep.

Create a restorative morning routine that includes prayer, meditation, and positive reading or media (podcasts, videos...)

Start with 7 days of consistent journaling (extending this writing practice 7 days at a time.)

Tell your story to a safe ear. Fnd someone (therapist, religious leader, best friend...) you can release your story to- someone who will hear you, see you, and feel you without judgement.

There was a time when I thought my life was trying to kill me.

One thing after another was coming at me.

Some business deals failed. I had a very difficult first pregnancy. The doctor said I had chronic kidney disease. My family and I relocated to another state- and landed in the middle of real-estate fraud...

I was having a really tough time.

I spent countless nights and early mornings trying to figure out what I had done wrong. I thought I was being punished, reaping something I had previously sown, experience the firm hand of karma...

One day I was talking to my mentor and she asked me if I was okay, just like she had countless times before. This time, I didn't just say, *yeah, I'm good*- just like I had countless times before.

This time I cried.

I cried... and cried some more.

She said it's okay. Cry if you need to.

Turns out I really needed to.

I didn't die that day (obviously.) I felt like I would. But, I didn't.

Life was hard. I needed a minute and I took it.

If you're not okay, say so.

If you're thinking about giving up, don't.
There's a new day waiting for you.

Word of advice:

When you come across a woman making her
way through a slow season, recovering after
a setback, or laying low while she tightens
things up a bit, don't count her out.

She's a real one.

One day it won't hurt as much.

I pray you heal from things no one has even apologized for.

If you never hear *I'm sorry*...
If they never say they were wrong...
If they never admit they hurt you...
If they never right their wrongs...

I pray you heal anyway.

It's making you better.

One day you are going to wake up to a brighter day. Your worry, doubt, and anxiety will be a thing of the past. You will be full of faith and depleted of all fear. You will be confident in who you are and amazed by the grace you've been given to endure long enough to win.

Until then, just keep going.

One day you are going to meet someone who sees you for who you really are and loves you even more. That someone is going to love everything you hate about yourself. That someone is going to inspire you to be better and support your every attempt.

Until then, don't settle.

One day you are going to understand every lesson that life has offered you.
One day you are going to see every struggle, setback, and disappointment as a blessing.
One day, the fight of your life will be seen as an opportunity of a lifetime.

-Be Encouraged

When you know who you are, so will everyone else.

People who have made the biggest mistakes
often have the brightest futures.

They know what not to do.

You are worth more than every mistake
you've ever made.

You gotta know you're worth the effort.

Lost the ability to hold on
Found the strength to let go

Lost my cool, mind was half gone
Found my peace in quiet places

The most beautiful things get found
when you're lost.

-Get Lost

...And if it never gets easy
I hope you'll just keep going
cause you'll get stronger.

You won't need easy, then.

Smile. Not because you ain't going through, but because want you're going through didn't break you.

I ain't survive the hood just to grow up and
let a little struggle shake me.

I get annoyed.
I get overwhelmed.
I get frustrated.
I get tired

Been knocked down.
Been counted out.
Been overlook.
Been unrated.

I've been through it all, with tears in my
eyes but a smile on face, because I knew it
wouldn't break me.

Shoutout to those going through with a
smile on your face.

I feel you...

I am learning that my peace is worth the chaos I gotta go through to get it.

You can't avoid the work that it takes to heal

You can't skip the process you gotta go through to get where you want to be.

You can't avoid talking about the trauma if you want to work through it.

You can't keep acting like you're alright when you're not.

The chaos of heart-work is excruciating at times, but the peace you get in exchange is worth it.

Work for your peace.
Protect your peace.
Honor your peace.

And reject anything that tries to steal it.

It took you 10, 20, 30 years to finally look in the mirror and be okay with what you see, to be confident in the decisions you've made.

Stop letting people wreck your whole life with a 5 minute conversation about what they think about your life.

This is hard when your mama nem' have
made themselves comfortable in your life.
It's difficult for some people to tell their best
friend to mind her business.

It's not easy not to let verbal attacks against
your calling effect how you move.

But if you're going to do this thing,
keep other people's opinions away from
your dreams.

Protect your purpose.

Build your life in silence and pursue the
desires of your heart in peace.

I know it's hard to believe that after so much
bad, good can actually happen.

But it can.

Holding on so tight to what you have for
fear of having nothing at all...

So many years of losing got you thinking
winning isn't even a possibility...

Settling because even the thought of trying
again gets you anxious...

You haven't left yourself open for anything
other than what you've had.

I know it's hard to believe that after so much
bad, good can even happen- but it can.

And if you keep healing, it will.

Dear Self,

You are everything your heart says you are.

You can accomplish all the things you see in your dreams.

Your light is as bright as you think it is.

You are not random.

There is purpose in your life.

Take extra care of yourself.
Choose the words you hear wisely.

Resuscitate those old dreams and untouched goals by speaking life and affirming what you want to see.

You are who you think you are.

You may never hear, I'm sorry.
They may never admit you were right.
He may never realize you were the one.
You will lose some, you will fail much.

You will take the hits, and you will recover.

One day is not a day of the week but a
moment in time.

When effort turs into result
When what you hoped for is what you have
When a prayer becomes a testimony...

One day it will all make sense.
One day it will be worth it.

One day you will look back on today and be
happy you never gave up.

Don't just wait for one day, look forward to
it.

It's coming.

May not always smile.
May get caught with a bad attitude.
May be a lot to handle.
May have layers to get through...

But even on your worst day, you are still
worthy of love.

Your issues, flaws, and shortcomings do not disqualify you.

You are still worthy.

What didn't happen wasn't supposed to.

Remember this as you reflect on your life:

There are things you weren't ready for.
There are things you were being protected
from.

There are things that don't belong to you.
There are people that are no good for you.

There are things that didn't happen- not
because you were rejected, overlooked, or
wasn't good enough got it.

It just wasn't supposed to happen.

At first the pain just hurt.

Then it taught me something
Then I grew from it
Then I shared my story of survival.

…And that is how I went from pain to
power.

Once you learn to turn pain into power,
everything changes.

You've been grieving over a loss that was
actually a rescue.

You've been granted a second chance.

You've been spared.
You've been protected.
You've been covered.

You thought you lost but if you shift your
perspective, you'll see what you've gained.

I hope this encourages you to finally let go.

What didn't happen wasn't supposed to.
What left your life wasn't yours.
What you lost is not the best you'll ever
have.

As you continue to make your way through,
and discover your losses were actually gains,
your next steps will get easier to take.

She realized that if she was going to become the woman she was meant to be, she had to do it on purpose.

She made a choice
Set some intentions
Took action, daily
And decided she was never going to
settle...

That's when everything changed.

The people who hurt you may not want to see you healed.

Working through healing your broken heart, your childhood trauma, your broken marriage, your strained relationships... Will exposed the people who caused it.

If you are still connected to those people, that may be difficult for them to face- especially if they are not doing their own work.

Understanding this will prevent you from being revictimized.

The other thing is: healing will cause you show up differently.

Things that used to be okay will no longer fly. Stuff you used to put up with will no longer be tolerated. People who used to get second chances will be cut off after the first offense.

The healed you understands the value of peace and wholeness and because you've worked so hard to get it, you're no longer putting it at risk.

The people who hurt you understand what that means for them. They may not want to see you healed, but heal anyway.

Fear will have you referring to your past.

Faith will have you rooting for your future.

Stay in faith.

When you're used to moving through life in pieces, being whole may feel like you're out of your own body at first.

Sit in your whole, Beloved.

It will feel like home soon.

What you just read will explain why setting boundaries makes you feel guilty.

It will answer your question about why accepting compliments is so difficult for you.

It will speak to your struggle to convey why you need time alone.

Keep setting those boundaries, letting love in, and doing what you need to take care...

It gets easier.

The part of you that still has scars is just as worthy.

A broken heart still has capacity for love.

A mind that feels lost can still remember who you were and imagine who you can be.

A body that's been afflicted can still carry life.

There is still value in the parts of you that haven't healed yet.

Heal so when you get what you've been
asking for, you can keep it.

Heal for your children's children.

Feel what you feel
until what you feel is healed.

How you feel is an expression of your heart, and outpouring from your circumstance, and/or a response to your life's experience.

As your heart heals, your circumstances change, and your life's experience evolve. So will your feelings.

And it is okay to feel what you feel until then.

Growing.

Some days I swear I'm gonna give up.

Some days I swear I'll never give up.

Some days I just swear.

Every day I just keep going.

What you are experiencing, right now,
could be answered prayer.

Be careful of what you grieve over.

Everything you lost is not a loss.
Every "no" was not rejection.
Every closed door was not opportunity lost.

What if you were being protected?
What if you were experiencing redirection?

What if you are being groomed, molded,
and shaped into the woman you'll need to
be in order to handle your real blessing?

What if things are falling apart not because
your life is hard, but because you've been
praying, really hard, for something better?

Check your prayer list, and see how things
align.

Stay ready.

When it's your turn, it won't matter where
you are in line.

People will wait in line for shoes, food, entertainment... Might complain the whole time if it's long or moving slow. But once you've waited, you get this "I ain't wait this long for nothing" kind of attitude, and you hold your space in line because eventually you know you'll be up next.

Such is life.

There are lines of people waiting to fulfill their purpose, waiting to use their gifts, waiting to express their talents, waiting to start their families, waiting to make some money, waiting to be heard, waiting to be who they were called to be- and sometimes the lines are long and move slow. But you gotta have enough conviction to hold your space in line down, no matter how long or how slow.

You ain't been praying, planning, hustling, and waiting this long for nothing.

Stay ready.

I can.
I will.
I did.

You don't need another resolution.
You need a declaration.

A formal announcement putting your life on notice of your intention to reject all doubt, all fear, all self-sabotage, all limiting beliefs, all settling, and all of anything else that would tempt you to live this year like you did the last... You don't need another New Year Resolution.

You need conviction.

A formal declaration that your future is certain. A firm belief that you can and will do whatever you set out to do.

This is my prayer, affirmation, mantra, and declaration:

I can.
I will.
I did...

What will you declare?

You're not overreacting.
You're not being unreasonable.
You're not reading into it too much.
You're not being extra.

Your intuition is speaking to you.
Listen up.

That feeling is your divine gift.

It's your guide. Your cheerleader. Your therapist. Your coach. Your wing (wo)man.

It's the voice that informs you when God has something to say.

When it speaks, be sure to listen. Let it resound over every other voice. Let it quiet the confusion. Let it utter sermons of encouragement, direction, and assurance.

Let the part of you that knows exactly what you need, speak.

-Intuition

Not sorry for anything I had to do to
become a better me.

Had to preserve my energy for what's important.

Didn't have time to engage in things that didn't move me forward.

Couldn't talk about the things I used to.

Wasn't feeling the same about the old days.

Found myself on a whole other vibe.

Spent hours praying with no time to spare on complaining.

Turned down invitations to pity parties.

Discovered a whole new way of being.

That made some people uncomfortable and that was the revelation I needed the most.

I'll ask you to excuse me while I become better, but what I won't do is apologize for it.

You know you've grown when you can
look back over the toughest time in your life
and not shed a tear.

You know you've changed when you can
look back on one of the worst days you've
experience and can't recall all the details.

You know you've learned the lesson when
you can teach it to someone else.

Some people just go through things,
and some people grow through things.

I used to think it didn't matter how you got
through, as long as you got through.

But I grew tired of getting to the other side,
still stuck at my starting point, emotionally.

When the dust cleared, I wanted to be still
standing- but not with a broken heart, not
with regret, not with unforgiveness, not with
depression... So I went to work- because
that's what it takes to get your healing.

If you're going to go through it, grow
through it. And when the dust clears, you'll
still be standing there- but with your healing.

Don't shrink to fit into a box that was never meant for you.

Don't waste your energy trying to figure out
why you feel out of place.

Your dreams are too big for the small minds
and small spaces you're trying to share them
with.

You're not too much.
The space you're trying to fit in is too small.

Don't shrink.

Build a space big enough to hold all of you
and leave the box behind.

There may be moments in life when what you do may make others uncomfortable.

Do it anyway.

Trust me, they will be alright.

Everyone tells you to live outside your comfort zone.

But no one reminds you not to create comfort zones for others to dwell in.

It's unfortunate that your best life is a threat to others.

It's a shame that some people can't stand the thought of you being blessed.

It's sad that some of the people in your life can't handle your growth.

But that's their issue, not yours.

Let me warn you right now: some people are about to be really uncomfortable with how you move in this season of your life.

Don't question your moves, question those people.

Too focused on the future to be distracted
by the past.

Grateful for all the things that went wrong,
for all the right reasons.

Clear up space.
Make room for something better.

Forgive yourself for the things you couldn't do.

Give yourself credit for the things you did well.

Ask for grace.

You'll need it to keep moving forward.

May you grow to realize,
some losses were gains.

Lost some relationships,
gained some peace.

Lost some opportunities,
gained some insight.

Made some mistakes,
learned some lessons.

You are never at a loss when you learn,
grow, and heal from it.

...And some things you thought were
adding to your life needed to be subtracted
so you could recognize your own value.

You are not at a loss as long as you still have
you.

God bless the old me.

She went through a lot to get me here.

Purpose is a powerful thing.

It will have you walking around in life like
you belong here.

Forgiveness doesn't mean you forget.

It means you are committed to accepting the fact that whatever happened, happened- and moving on with your life.

There is a lot of talk about how short life is.

Some people suggest you call loved ones to patch up broken relationships.

Some people comment on how those relationships never should have been broken in the first place because "blood is thicker than water," "family over everything," and "you only get one mom or dad."

I have lived through enough messy family stuff to know it's not that simple.

And I am actually against making decisions to repair anything based solely off emotions from fear of death or any other emotions for that matter. Never make a decision from a place of fear.

I am, however, here for forgiveness.

Forgiveness is accepting that you can not change what has already happened and making a conscious decision to move forward and keep living anyway- to decide not to carry hurt, or hate, or ill-will around with you because it only ends up resting in your heart, ultimately.

Forgiveness doesn't have to be a phone call or a family dinner that welcomes the people that hurt you back into your life.

It can be a silent choice to accept that what happened, happened- and live well anyway.

Life is short.

But if you live it well, it can be meaningful despite all the messy stuff.

Don't let anything block your blessing.

Be that:
I got this
I can do this
I can handle this
I can change this
I can do all things…

Kind of woman.

She's just not built to quit.

You've survived, outgrown, and outlasted things that should have taken you out.

Remember that the next time you doubt yourself.

Every now and then you have to check your own record just to remind yourself who you are.

You have to go back in your history, scroll through your story, and highlight the pages that detail your moments of overcoming, the days you didn't given up, and the times you pulled through with little to no scars.

But, even the scars are a reminder of what you've healed from.

You've survived too much to doubt yourself now.

Check your record.

This next version of you may scare some
people away.

Good.

This will explain a lot.

This is the answer to your questions about why people have been avoiding you, treating you differently, and making you feel like you're the one acting strange:

Growth makes people who want to stay the same feel a way.

That's on them, not you.

You are not obligated to remain the same
version of yourself that's stuck inside
someone else's mind.

Time to release yourself from expectations other people place on you.

Time to be okay with outgrowing some people.

Time to remind yourself that who you are, for real, is worth giving up who you pretend to be.

Time to shine no matter who can't stand your light.

Time to grow into yourself without fear of other people's opinions.

You are not the same.

And that's a good thing, since growth is your goal.

Spent years doubting myself.

I'm done with that now.

Doubt will have you thinking that because of your past:

You can't finish what you've started
You're not worthy of something better
You can't create something good
Your life will remain the same...

Don't believe your doubt or anything else that is stuck in your past.

Who you are today and where you're headed is on a whole new energy.

You can and you will finish what you've started, experience something better, create something good, and continue to grow into a version of yourself that you and your past has never seen.

Be done with doubt and stay in faith.

Growth is a powerful thing.

It will have you walking around in life self-aware, letting things go, responding instead of reacting, and not taking everything personal.

This has been and, in many ways, still is the hardest thing for me to grow through.

When I feel wronged, hurt, offended, or disrespected my initial response is to lash out, to pop off, to set people straight.

What ends up happening is that in my lashing out, popping off, and setting people straight, it seems every time I've ever felt wronged, hurt, offended, and disrespected resurfaces- and I unleash the pain of unhealed scares on who's ever present.

Have you ever been in a position where you felt compelled to apologize to an offender because your reaction was way out of pocket?

I have prayed and worked for healing and growth in this area, for years.

And one day, while in the middle of a heated discussion, I felt myself wanting to unleash- but instead I resigned myself to my desire to become the best version of me- and shut. my. mouth. Literally, mid-sentence I let out a "you know what: I'm good, love," ended my contribution to the conversation- and it actually felt good to do so in that moment.

That is growth.

I am still working out what to do with what I feel. But when I show growth in this way, what I feel in the moment doesn't last as long.

Healing is work.
Growth is work.

But becoming a better version of me is worth the effort.

You are worth growing for.

Soft is not weak.
Quiet is not mute.
Still is not stagnant.

There is a difference.

Sometimes the fight of your life is an internal battle, won through prayer, reflection, and healing.

Sometimes the revelation is made evident by the things you don't say.

Sometimes rest and calm is what you need to keep going.

You can show strength, have a voice, and make progress, even in your slow seasons.

And just like that
she was over it.

No more tears.
No more sleepless nights.
No more self-doubt.

She pulled herself together
and never look back.

-Tired

It can happen just like that.

In a moment of clarity
you can make a firm decision to be done,
and really be done.

You'll have to hold yourself accountable.
You may be tempted to question your
decision.

But there's an energy that accompanies being
done, that just hits different.

You may not be where you want to be, doing the things you want to do, with the people you want to do them with, but you're on your way.

This is just part of your story.

The rest is still unwritten.

But every part of your story, and every version of you is valid.

I see you.

Shoutout to the loud-mouth woman who found her voice and uses it to inspire other women to find theirs. We need you.

To the woman who isn't afraid to be alone long enough to discover her own identity, measure her true value, and cultivate the kind of genuine self-love that won't get lost when loving someone else, you inspire.

To the woman who found her purpose after losing relationships, time, money, and almost her sanity, remember what you lost is not the best you'll ever have.

To the woman who is still trying to find her way, getting tired of trusting the process, and unsure of her purpose here on earth, you are exactly where you need to be to become that girl who leaps above circumstance and lands on her feet.

I see all of you.

Made in the USA
Coppell, TX
19 November 2020

41641974R00104